MICROLIFE

THE MICROSCOPIC WORLD
OF TINY CREATURES

MICROLIFE

THE MICROSCOPIC WORLD
OF TINY CREATURES

By
David Burnie

Consultant
Marek Walisiewicz

A Dorling Kindersley Book

Dorling **DK** Kindersley

LONDON, NEW YORK, MUNICH,
MELBOURNE, and DELHI

Project Editor Steve Setford
Project Art Editor Peter Radcliffe
Senior Editor Fran Jones
Senior Art Editor Stefan Podhorodecki
Category Publisher Linda Martin
Managing Art Editor Jacquie Gulliver
Picture Researcher Marie Osborn
DK Picture Library Charlotte Oster, Gemma Woodward,
Jonathan Brooks
Production Jenny Jacoby
DTP Designer Siu Yin Ho

First published in Great Britain in 2002 by
Dorling Kindersley Limited
80 Strand, London WC2R 0RL

2 4 6 8 10 9 7 5 3 1

The CIP Catalogue record for this book is available
from the British Library

ISBN 0-7513-3920-2

Reproduced by Colourscan, Singapore
Printed and bound by L.E.G.O., Italy

See our complete
catalogue at
www.dk.com

CONTENTS

INTRODUCTION

Because humans are so smart, it's easy to imagine that we're top of the class in the natural world. But being big and clever is only one route to success – being small and simple is another, and it's the survival plan used by microlife. These tiny specks of life have been around for much longer than we have, and they outnumber us by at least a trillion trillion trillion times!

If you've got good eyesight, the smallest thing you can see will be about one-tenth the size of this full stop. This book is about the creatures that you can't see in any detail, and about the ones that live in the microworld. As you'll discover, they are even more varied than the things we come across in daily life, and many of them are a lot tougher as well. In fact, wherever humans venture on Earth, microlife turns out to have got there first, from snowy mountains to the ocean floor, and even deep inside the Earth.

TARDIGRADES, OR "WATER BEARS", ARE TINY ANIMALS THAT CAN SURVIVE FOR YEARS WITHOUT FOOD OR WATER.

Many of these microscopic lifeforms are only ever seen by scientists, which is why they don't have well-known names. But their small size doesn't mean that we should ignore them, because some can make us very sick or even kill us. Luckily, we have far more friends than enemies in this invisible world. The truth is, we actually need microlife to survive.

If you want to explore the subject in more detail, check out the Log On "bites" that appear throughout this book. These will direct you to some fascinating websites where you can find out even more about the inhabitants of the microworld. So dive in, and be ready to meet some weird and wonderful creatures!

David Burnie

INVISIBLE WORLD

When people first started using microscopes, about 400 years ago, they were amazed – and sometimes horrified – to discover that the Earth teems with tiny living things. Since then, microscopes have become much more powerful, and so we know a lot more about what goes on in the world of microlife. And guess what? The closer you zoom in, the smaller and stranger it gets!

Down and down!

The microworld is a bewildering place, particularly when it comes to the important matter of size.

To get your bearings, imagine you're stepping into a lift that will take you down into the microworld. But this is not an ordinary lift, because as it goes down, it also reduces you in size. On each floor, you'll meet things that are roughly 10 times smaller than those on the floor above.

HYDRA LOOK LIKE ALIENS FROM SPACE, BUT THEY LIVE IN PONDS AND USE THEIR TENTACLES TO CATCH FOOD.

PARAMECIUM

DIDINIUM

So here goes! The lift drops, and the doors open to reveal the inhabitants of floor number one. As you take a quick look around, you see a host of animals, such as water fleas and *Hydra*, all built on a miniature scale. Some creatures flutter by on minute wings, while others crawl or swim past. A few look familiar, which isn't so surprising, because they are all more than 1 mm (0.04 in) long. That's about the size of a pinhead, meaning that you're not yet in the microworld. The real entrance to the microworld is on the floor below.

The land of single cells
When you step out on floor number two, things have a

A PREDATORY PROTIST CALLED DIDINIUM (BROWN) ATTACKS PARAMECIUM (BLUE), ANOTHER PROTIST. DIDINIUM'S SNOUT IS OPENING TO ENGULF ITS VICTIM.

more alien feel. There are still plenty of animals about, but because they are so small – no more than one-tenth the size of the creatures you've just met – they're not ones that you're likely to have seen before.

However, most of the things on floor two aren't animals at all, and they don't have real bodies as such. Instead, they are protists – simple organisms, neither true animals nor true plants, that consist of just a single cell. A few protists are big enough to be visible with the naked eye, but most of them are micro-organisms. In other

9

live by gathering the energy in light. *Chlorella* itself measures 0.015 mm (0.0006 in) across. Lined up side by side, it would take 70 *Chlorella* to stretch across a full stop.

Halfway house

After you have said goodbye to *Chlorella*, the lift drops again and you pass through another frontier. From here onwards, living things are at least 1,000 times smaller than they were on floor one. Not only that, but they're also much simpler, because their cells are too small to contain lots of different parts. But as you discover when the doors slide apart on floor number four, simple doesn't necessarily mean unsuccessful. In fact, quite the reverse…floor four turns out to be absolutely teeming with life.

Bugs and germs

At this level, the microworld is dominated by bacteria – or, if you prefer it, bugs and germs. Like chocolates, bacteria come in a range of shapes, but they're covered in some distinctly unpleasant outer coatings, from lanky hairs to gooey slime!

CHLORELLA IS THE GREEN DUST THAT GETS ON YOUR CLOTHES WHEN YOU CLIMB TREES. IT'S ALSO FOUND IN PUDDLES AND PONDS.

words, you'd normally need a microscope to see them.

Going green

With the entrance to the microworld safely behind you, it's down to floor number three. When the doors open here, they reveal the smallest living things that have complex cells like the ones in our own bodies. Among the residents of floor three are tiny algae. These are plant-like lifeforms, such as *Chlorella*, that

Most of them spend their entire lives in one place, but as you soon find out, some of them can swim, and they zoom past at amazing speed. Floor four is clearly not a place to hang around for very long. Although things that are made up of cells, and also the smallest things on Earth that can be thought of as genuinely alive. They can be just 0.0002 mm (0.000008 in) across, which means that a full stop would

MICROLIFE OUTNUMBERS VISIBLE LIFE BY OVER 10 BILLION TO ONE

most of the world's bacteria are to be found on the fourth floor, the smallest of them – called mycoplasmas – are waiting at your next stop, floor five. These micro-microbes are the smallest have room for about 5,000 mycoplasmas side by side.

The edge of life
Mycoplasmas are just about visible with the most powerful

THIS EERIE OUTLINE IS MADE UP OF BILLIONS OF BACTERIA THAT WERE LIVING ON A PERSON'S HAND.

light microscopes, which can magnify objects by up to 2,000 times. But beyond this point, light waves are too clumsy to pick out anything smaller, and beams of electrons or X-rays have to be used instead. These can reveal far more detail, magnifying 100,000 times or more. And that's how scientists know about what lurks on the sixth floor.

You are now in virus territory, a weird and barely imaginable world where tiny packages of chemicals can actually come to life. Large viruses may be as long as mycoplasmas, although they are always much more slender. But most viruses are far smaller, and some are only 0.000017 mm (0.00000067 in) across. Viruses can't survive unless they invade living cells. Because of this, they barely qualify as living things at all – unlike everything else you've met so far.

Journey's end

Once the lift drops below the sixth floor, things are at least a million times smaller than they were on floor one. This is too small for anything to have even a flicker of life, so we are left looking at individual chemicals.

The seventh floor contains "macromolecules". These are complicated substances, such as DNA, which contains all the chemical instructions needed to make living things. Most of these macromolecules contain several hundred atoms, and sometimes many more. On the eighth floor there are simpler chemicals like glucose, which has just 24 atoms.

Finally, on the ninth floor, the lift comes to a halt – it's your last stop. This level is filled with individual atoms, which are the smallest complete pieces of matter inside living things.

Between the start of your journey and the ninth floor, there's been a change in scale of exactly one billion times. Your introductory tour is now complete. Don't bother with farewells, as you'll meet many of these odd characters later on. It's time to go back up in the lift, to meet the drifters of the microworld.

THIS IS JUST A TINY PART OF A DNA MOLECULE.

DNA IS FOUND IN ALL LIVING CELLS. MOLECULES OF DNA WORK A BIT LIKE COMPUTER PROGRAMS, EXCEPT THEIR INSTRUCTIONS ARE WRITTEN IN A CHEMICAL CODE.

LIFE ADRIFT

Life began in the sea, so it's no surprise that this is where microlife is most abundant and diverse. Some of these organisms live on the ocean floor, but many more spend all their lives adrift. Together they make up the plankton – a floating world that's like a watery soup. But it's a soup with a difference, because the "bits" in it are alive!

Mysterious migrants

During World War II, sailors searching for enemy submarines found something menacing on their sonar screens – a gigantic object hovering above the ocean floor. In the daytime, it was about 500 m (1,640 ft) down, but towards sunset it started to rise. By nightfall, the object had almost surfaced, and at this point the anxious sub-hunters rushed outside to look.

PLANKTON INCLUDES TINY SEA ANIMALS THAT START THEIR LIVES AS LARVAE.

But nothing was there. Or at least, that's how it seemed until marine biologists took a closer look at the water itself and found that it was swarming with tiny animals. Oil droplets in the creatures' bodies had reflected the sonar signals, making it look as though something enormous was on the move.

The moving zoo

These tiny migrants are called zooplankton, and they form the busiest part of the drifting world. The "zoo" bit doesn't mean that they are looked after by keepers – instead, it just shows that they are animals rather than plants. Zooplankton includes young fish and shrimp-like copepods not much bigger than a human fingernail, together with a host of smaller minibeasts. For them, the daily swim to the surface is equivalent to a person walking

40 km (25 miles). So why on Earth do they bother to do it?

Ocean commuters

The answer is food. Many of these animals sift their food from the water, and the things that most of them catch are phytoplankton, or microscopic drifting plants. Phytoplankton soak up the energy in sunlight,

WEIRD WORLD

SOME PLANKTONIC ANIMALS CAN LIGHT UP AFTER DARK. NOCTILUCA MAY SWITCH ON ITS LIGHT IF DISTURBED BY A BOAT. WHEN PLENTIFUL, NOCTILUCA MAKES A BOAT'S BOW WAVE LOOK AS THOUGH IT'S ON FIRE!

This long trek also shields them from bright sunlight, which can sometimes damage their bodies.

staying close to the surface where the light is brightest. To collect enough of these tiny sun-lovers, planktonic animals

Growing up

Most of the zooplankton that make this up-and-down journey are at least 1 cm (0.4 in) long.

PLANKTON IS THE FOOD THAT FUELS ANIMAL LIFE IN THE SEAS

have to be at the surface too. But there's a catch – during the day, the surface swarms with fish that swallow zooplankton whole. To avoid ending up in a fishy belly, many planktonic animals hide down in the depths during the day, and only swim upwards at dusk.

But plankton also teems with much smaller animals – ones that don't have the strength to shuttle back and forth. Most of them are short-term drifters. They live in the plankton when they are young, but alter their appearance and lifestyle as they grow up. These floating youngsters can't be accused of looking like their parents. In fact, many look so different it's hard to believe they're related at all. Adult barnacles, for example, live their lives

BARNACLE LARVA

sticks up out of their back, while young sea urchins look like microscopic satellites, complete with a set of antennae. Family likeness? No way!

Drifting off

These bizarre babies are called larvae, and they have a very important role to play. During their time in the plankton, they can drift hundreds or even

A BARNACLE LARVA (LEFT) IS A PLANKTONIC DRIFTER. ADULT BARNACLES (BELOW) ANCHOR THEMSELVES FIRMLY TO ROCKS USING AN INCREDIBLY STRONG "GLUE".

stuck to rocks, and are protected by a thick outer case that looks like a shell. But their babies have a cluster of feathery legs, a single eye, and no trace of a "shell" at all. Similarly, young crabs are very un-crablike, with slender tails and a hooked spike that thousands of kilometres. In the final stages of growing up, young crabs and sea urchins drop down to the sea floor and then scuttle away or creep off towards their final homes.

But junior barnacles have a trickier, riskier task ahead.

Touch down

As adults, barnacles spend their days firmly cemented to solid rock. But it can't be any old rock. Instead, it has to be one on the shore, in the right kind of water, and at just the right height between the tides. When it comes to selecting a rock, a barnacle youngster doesn't get a second chance. Once it has cemented itself in place, it's stuck for good, so a wrong choice would mean certain death.

When a likely rock comes within range, the larva carries out a whole battery of checks, as it sizes up its potential home. But one thing clinches the decision. If the larva detects chemicals from adult barnacles,

CERATIUM IS IS ONE OF THE WORLD'S MOST DANGEROUS DRIFTING ALGAE, BECAUSE IT CAN RELEASE A DEADLY POISON INTO THE WATER.

SPINNING FLAGELLUM

DRIVING FLAGELLUM

it knows that it has found a good place to live. As long as there's room to spare on the rock, it touches down, and gets ready to glue itself in place.

In the swim

If you think that only animals can swim, you're in for a big surprise. Some planktonic algae, or "micro-plants", are just as good at speeding along. One of the strangest of these is

Ceratium. It's only 0.5 mm (0.02 in) long – roughly the amount your fingernails grow in a week – but when magnified, it looks like a spiky helmet from an ancient suit of armour. *Ceratium* moves by beating two microscopic hairs, called flagella, set at right angles to each other. One flagellum spins it round, while the other drives it forwards. With one of its spikes leading the way, *Ceratium* whirls its way through the sea.

THIS RED TIDE IN NEW ZEALAND CONTAINS BILLIONS OF POISONOUS ALGAE.

R ed and dead

Most planktonic algae are harmless to humans…but not all. In warm parts of the world, *Ceratium* and its relatives can be deadly. These algae sometimes undergo population explosions, creating "red tides" that stain the sea reddish-brown. Red tides look bad and smell worse, and they are awash with powerful poisons, which the algae release around them. Some of these poisons are lethal to fish, but the ones most dangerous to humans don't actually harm fish at all. Instead, they get stored in

THOUSANDS OF DEAD LOBSTERS WASHED ASHORE AFTER A RED TIDE ARE BEING BULLDOZED AWAY.

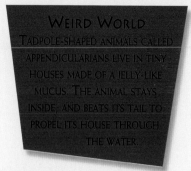

the bodies of fish, clams and other sea creatures, turning them into living booby-traps. Every year, people in these areas die from eating this toxic seafood – sometimes just one bite can be lethal.

The micro-predators

Micro-plants swim to keep near the light, and also to escape single-celled hunters searching for a meal. These minute but greedy creatures include a galaxy of tiny predators that snare or engulf their food. One of the most common, called *Globigerina*, catches its food with the help of gooey "fishing lines" that it spreads out around its collection of bubble-shaped shells. When anything brushes against one of the lines it becomes stuck fast. *Globigerina* quickly pulls in its catch and starts to digest it.

Just as scary are the hunters known as radiolarians, which include some giants of the single-celled world. Surrounded by spikes and invisible threads, they trap anything edible that they touch. They are a deadly

AS GLOBIGERINA DRIFTS ALONG, IT TRAWLS FOR FOOD WITH ITS "FISHING LINES".

THIS AMAZING STRUCTURE IS THE DEAD SKELETON OF A RADIOLARIAN – A MICROSCOPIC PREDATOR SMALLER THAN A DUST SPECK.

danger to algae, and they mop up millions of tonnes each year. Fortunately for us, the biggest of these hunter-killers is just a few millimetres across!

Secret skeletons

In water, just as on land, it helps to stay in shape. Planktonic plants often do this with an outer coating made of cellulose, while planktonic animals often have hard parts made of calcium carbonate, which is also found in human bones. But some single-celled creatures, including radiolarians, use a very different building material – glass. A glass skeleton might sound a dangerous thing to have, and it certainly would be if it was built on a human scale. But if you are microscopic and are buoyed up by water, glass has a lot in its favour. Its chief ingredient, silica, is easy to find because it's dissolved in the sea. Better still, small pieces of glass are surprisingly strong, and they can be "grown" into an incredible variety of shapes.

21

sculptures. But these creatures aren't the only ones that use glass as a building material. Algae called diatoms are just as good at coming up with breathtaking designs. There are at least 5,000 different types of diatom, and they're found in freshwater as well as in the sea. Diatoms make cases with two almost-equal halves that fit together like the top and bottom of a box. Each case is peppered with an intricate pattern of struts and weight-saving holes, and the diatom's soft centre is tucked away inside. Diatom cases are so well built

MAGNIFIED OVER 1,000 TIMES, THESE DIATOM SKELETONS LOOK LIKE COINS THAT HAVE MELTED IN THE SUN.

S culptures in glass
Radiolarian skeletons are among the most beautiful objects in the seas. Some look like tiny sunbursts with spines and hooks, while others are more like futuristic

that they rarely break. They are also so small it would take 10 billion diatoms, side by side, to cover the front of this book.

P lankton from the past

When these tiny organisms die, their shells, cases, and skeletons tumble down to the seabed. Despite their size, they are so numerous that they build up like drifts of microscopic snow. The result is a deep layer of seabed ooze. This ooze can be many metres thick, but it builds up very slowly. In some parts of the ocean, it takes 100 years to add just the thickness of this page! Over many millions of years, the ooze is squashed and the skeletons become fossilized in solid rock. If the seabed is forced upwards, or if the sea level falls, the rock turns into dry land. Next time you pick up a piece of chalk or limestone, give it a closer look – you'll have ancient planktonic life in the palm of your hand!

LOG ON...
http://ebiomedia.com/gall/gallery_main.html

THESE CHALK CLIFFS ARE MADE UP OF MICROSCOPIC PLANKTON SKELETONS.

GERM ALERT

No matter how clean you think you are, your body teems with bacteria, and so does almost everything else around you. But don't panic, because apart from a few bad guys, most bacteria – or "germs" – are either helpful or quite harmless. These tiny organisms are the smallest things that are fully alive. They thrive in every habitat you can imagine…and a few that you probably can't.

Back to basics

If you enlarged a needle to the size of a broomstick, any bacteria on it would be only just visible to the naked eye. Bacteria each consist of a single cell. But because they are so small, there is no room for all the parts that keep other cells alive. Bacteria get by with just the basics – and they have been doing it with unbelievable success for over 3 billion years!

Bacteria can't see, can't hear, and don't have much of a social life. Most important of all, they can't swallow food, because they have nothing to swallow with. Instead, most bacteria live by digesting the things around them, and then soaking up the result. The easiest way to understand this is to imagine your skin is your stomach. To feed, all you'd need to do would be to lie down on your lunch!

THIS PICTURE SHOWS THE TIP OF A NEEDLE MAGNIFIED MANY TIMES. THE ORANGE SPECKS ARE BACTERIA.

ROD-SHAPED
BACILLUS BACTERIA

IN THIS "GALLERY OF GERMS" YOU CAN SEE
EXAMPLES OF THE THREE MAIN BACTERIA
SHAPES – ROD-SHAPED, ROUND, AND SPIRAL.

Sticky moments

There are at least 10,000 types
of bacteria, but because they
are so simple, they are not as
varied as other living things.
They come in just three basic
shapes – rod-shaped, round, or
spiral – although a few real
eccentric characters are star-
shaped or square.

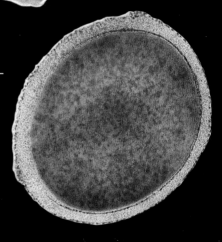

ROUND MICROCOCCUS BACTERIUM

Bacteria have a very simple
structure. Inside a bacterium is
a jelly-like cytoplasm containing
chemicals that help it to work
and grow. Around this is a thin
membrane that controls which
substances enter or leave the
cell. In most bacteria, this is
surrounded by a rigid cell wall
and a sticky, slimy outer jacket
that protects them from attack

SPIRAL LEPTOSPIRA
BACTERIUM

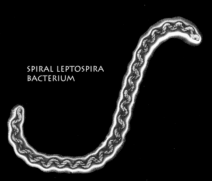

25

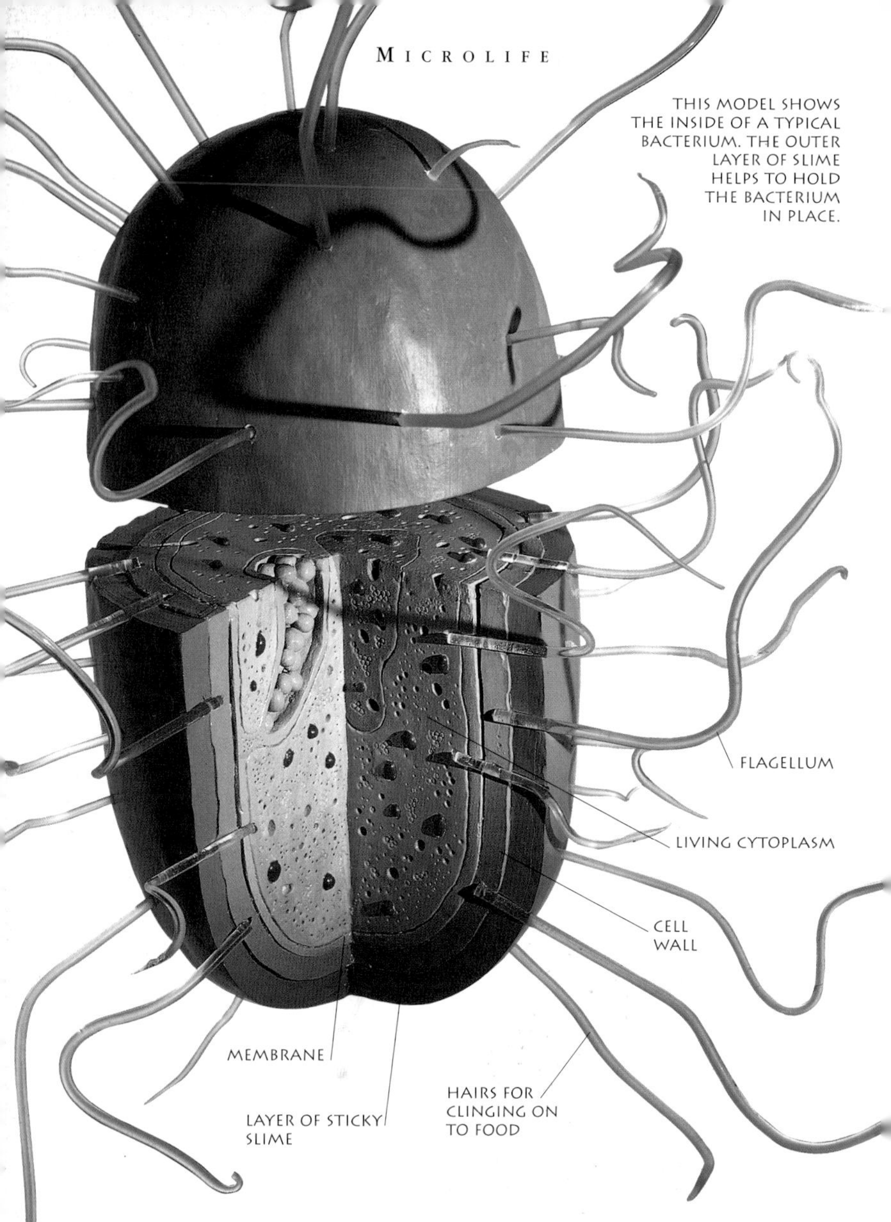

THIS MODEL SHOWS
THE INSIDE OF A TYPICAL
BACTERIUM. THE OUTER
LAYER OF SLIME
HELPS TO HOLD
THE BACTERIUM
IN PLACE.

FLAGELLUM

LIVING CYTOPLASM

CELL
WALL

MEMBRANE

HAIRS FOR
CLINGING ON
TO FOOD

LAYER OF STICKY
SLIME

and stops them from drying out. This adhesive coat also allows them to glue themselves firmly in place. The glue is extremely strong, and it makes bacteria difficult to dislodge once they've found a suitable feeding spot. It explains why just giving the kitchen worktop a quick wipe won't make it bacteria-free…even though it may look sparkling and clean.

LOG ON...
Take a museum tour at
www.bacteriamuseum.org

Picky eaters

Bacteria "eat" a mind-boggling range of different things, but individually they are very fussy about their diet. For example, the bacteria that live on human teeth – and there are more than 300 types – feed on sugars and eat virtually nothing else. Other specialists eat mainly proteins or fats, which they get either from living things or from dead remains. And there are even bacteria that can tackle the most unsavoury-sounding foods, with soap, shoe polish, and crude oil all appearing on the menu. Yuk!

All these foods have one thing in common – they contain substances made by other organisms. But some bacteria manage to get the energy they need to survive without having to rely on other living things. They do this either by absorbing energy directly from sunlight, or by collecting dissolved chemicals that bubble up from deep underground, and using them for chemical reactions that release energy.

Toughing it

Scientists have found bacteria high up in the atmosphere, and also several kilometres below the surface of the Earth. Bacteria are also found everywhere in-between, from forests, kitchens, and bathrooms, to the bottom of the sea. They can put up with the most extreme conditions, and actually flourish in glaciers and hot springs, where other living things would either freeze or cook.

Live-in partners

Bacteria can live inside plants, often in small bumps on their roots. Called root nodules, the

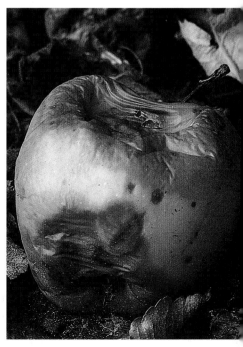

BACTERIA DEVOURING THIS APPLE HAVE CAUSED IT TO TURN BROWN AND ROT.

WEIRD WORLD

ONE OF THE WORLD'S DEADLIEST POISONS IS MADE BY *CLOSTRIDIUM BOTULINUM*, A BACTERIUM THAT LIVES IN THE SOIL. ONE DROP OF THIS COULD KILL 100,000 PEOPLE! LUCKILY, CONTACT WITH THIS POISON IS RARE.

bumps contain bacteria that collect nitrogen from air in the soil and change it into a form that plants can use. Nitrogen is essential for plant growth, and their nodules work like tiny fertilizer factories, enabling them to thrive. In return, the bacteria get a safe place to live, as well as some of the sugar in the plants' sap to eat. It's an example of symbiosis, which is a working partnership between two different types of living thing.

Us and them

There are about 100,000 billion bacteria living on and inside the average healthy person – that's about 10 times more than the body's own cells. Many are on the skin, while others inhabit the damp membranes that line our noses, mouths, and throats. A few even set up home on the conjunctiva – the tear-washed layer that covers our eyes.

However, the most popular address by far is the digestive system. Some particularly tough bacteria can cope with acids in the stomach, but most live in the intestines, where conditions are perfect. There's a constant supply of food and moisture, and the surroundings are cosy, with the temperature always a balmy 37°C (98.6°F). Not surprisingly, intestinal bacteria grow and reproduce at a staggering rate.

BACTERIA STICK TO INTESTINAL WALL.

IN HOSPITAL, STERILIZED INSTRUMENTS, CLOTHES, AND MASKS PREVENT PATIENTS FROM GETTING BACTERIAL INFECTIONS.

Bacteria inside you feed on the body's leftovers and waste products, and in most cases do no harm. Even if you could get rid of them all, it wouldn't be such a good idea, as some bacteria make vitamins that the body can use. And because there's so many of them, there's little space for less-desirable visitors to check in.

Trouble-makers

Bacteria don't have a rule book, so some of these guests occasionally stray from their rightful place. One frequent culprit is *Staphylococcus aureus*, which usually lives in the lining of the nose. If it gets into cuts, it can cause serious infections. This bacterium is a major problem in hospitals, because it is difficult to treat with drugs.

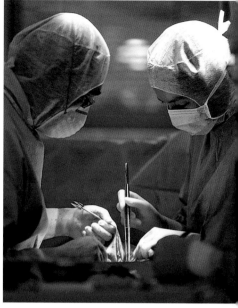

Bacteria can also cause us problems when they stay at home. *Escherichia coli*, or *E. coli* for short, lives in the intestines and is the commonest of the body's bacteria. "Normal" *E. coli* is very well-behaved, but some strains of this bacterium aren't so nice to have aboard. When swallowed in food or

DESTROYED CELLS

SOME E. COLI STRAINS RELEASE HARMFUL CHEMICALS THAT DAMAGE THE LINING OF THE INTESTINES, CAUSING BLOODY DIARRHOEA.

LINING OF THE INTESTINE

drinks, they trigger off bloody diarrhoea – very nasty!

Breaking and entering

Apart from these unfortunate exceptions, our body's bacteria generally lead fairly blameless lives. The same can't be said of pathogenic bacteria, which make a habit of causing disease. If they establish a foothold inside of us, these invaders can create real damage, and they do it in two different ways. Some pathogens cause trouble when they break into human cells, but many more wreak havoc by releasing poisons, or toxins, that circulate around the body in the blood. Some of these toxins are quite weak, and just make people feel out-of-sorts. However, a few are among the most powerful poisons in the world. The bacteria that make them aren't particularly rare – and chances are that some are just a few minutes' walk from where you are sitting now.

Fighting back

This alarming news might make you think twice before you next go out. But there's little need to worry, because the human body has a battery of defences

THESE WHOOPING COUGH BACTERIA ARE NESTLING IN A FOREST OF FINE HAIRS THAT LINE A PERSON'S THROAT.

WHITE BLOOD CELLS ARE PART OF THE IMMUNE SYSTEM. THIS ONE IS ATTACKING HARMFUL BACTERIA (RED).

against bacterial disease. The first line of defence is the skin, which most bacteria find very difficult to breach. If bacteria do manage to penetrate the skin barrier, then defence number two – the immune system – immediately comes into play.

The immune system has two sets of weapons – roving cells that gobble up invaders, and chemicals called antibodies that lock on to intruders, and sometimes the toxins that they produce. The immune system never forgets a face, and if an intruder stages a second attack, it strikes back even faster. Vaccinations are a way of priming the immune system to repel invaders. A vaccination introduces bacteria or toxins that have been made harmless, so that the body can prepare antibodies against the real thing. With these antibodies up your sleeve, you'll be well protected against future attack.

BACTERIA WERE THE FIRST LIVING THINGS TO DEVELOP ON EARTH

31

VIRUS ATTACK

I f you've got a cold, it might help to know that you're not alone. In fact, about 100 million people around the world are snuffling and sneezing their way through colds at this very moment. This all-too-familiar disease is just one of dozens produced by viruses – microscopic marauders that break into living cells and take over their controls.

Ready for action

Viruses are easy to muddle up with bacteria, but you won't make that mistake once you've discovered just how seriously weird they really are. Think of a tiny package of chemicals that can somehow come to life, and you'll have a good idea of what the average virus is like. Viruses are so small that they make bacteria look big and clumsy, which is quite a feat considering that bacteria themselves are invisible. And unlike all other microlife, viruses aren't made of cells, and they can't reproduce on their own. Instead, they are parasites, and they spring into life the moment a likely victim comes their way.

A SNEEZE CAN SHOWER COLD AND FLU VIRUSES QUITE A DISTANCE THROUGH THE AIR IN DROPLETS OF MUCUS.

Shaping up

Because viruses are so tiny, they are more like micro-machines than living things. Each one is built from a handful of standard parts, which fit together in a very precise way. For example, a typical cold virus has an outer case with 20 triangular sides, which meet at exactly 12 corners. When it's fully assembled, it looks more like a model that's been designed during a maths class than something that is really alive.

Flu viruses are rather more complicated, because they have an outer wrapper covered in tiny bumps, while bacteriophage viruses are trickier still. They come equipped with a case, a stalk, and six spindly "legs", making them resemble microscopic spacecraft.

Life on hold

Tucked away inside every virus is a hidden cargo – a program written in chemical code. But what's it for? Well, this program contains all the instructions needed to build more viruses, but it can only work once it is inside a living cell. Until that happens, the program cannot start, and the virus does nothing at all. It's not the kind

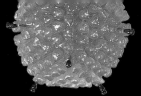

COLD VIRUSES (BLUE) CAN SURVIVE ON HOUSEHOLD OBJECTS, SO YOU CAN CATCH A COLD JUST BY OPENING A DOOR.

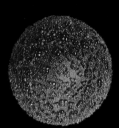

FLU VIRUSES (GREEN) ARE WRAPPED IN A FLEXIBLE MEMBRANE THAT HELPS THEM TO STICK TO LIVING CELLS.

of nothing that you do when you are having a boring time at home. Instead, the virus doesn't show even the faintest traces of life. But the instant the virus

WEIRD WORLD

MOST FLU EPIDEMICS START WHEN HUMAN VIRUSES AND ANIMAL VIRUSES (USUALLY FROM PIGS AND BIRDS) SWAP PARTS. THIS PRODUCES NEW FLU VIRUSES THAT THE HUMAN BODY CAN'T RECOGNIZE.

BACTERIOPHAGES LOOK LIKE MACHINES, BUT THEY HAVE NO MOVING PARTS. THEY RELY ON LUCK TO FIND THEIR TARGET.

"HEAD" INJECTS CHEMICAL PROGRAM INTO CELL.

"LEGS" GRIP CELL FIRMLY.

touches something living, it can suddenly switch itself on.

On target

If a virus makes contact with a target cell, it locks itself in place, and then slips its chemical program inside. This is the start of a micro "hijack" that will turn the new home into a virus assembly line. Viruses don't just invade any cell. Each type of virus has its own hit list of targets. For example, cold and flu viruses attack the cells that line the upper part of your throat – a favourite route for viruses to get into the human body.

THESE BACTERIOPHAGE VIRUSES HAVE LANDED ON A BACTERIUM, AND ARE ABOUT TO TAKE IT OVER.

You won't be surprised to hear that bacteriophages attack bacteria. But viruses play fair, and don't just victimize humans and bacteria. There are viruses that pick on all other lifeforms as well, from trees to whales. Some viruses can "jump" between species, but most stick to just one. That's why if you catch a cold, your pet hamster is unlikely to catch it too.

LOG ON... http://micro.magnet.fsu.edu/cells/virus.html

bacteria, viruses can't grow, so these virus "babies" are already full size.

Making a move

Now that they've left home, the new viruses need to spread out so that they can infect cells themselves. But viruses can't move, so they have to hitch a ride on something that's going their way. Cold viruses do this by stowing away in the sticky mucus that gives you a runny nose. When you have a good sneeze, droplets of mucus are sprayed into the air, carrying their tiny passengers far and wide. To catch "your" cold, other people simply have to breathe in the mucus droplets – something that's difficult to avoid.

Takeover bid

Once a virus has locked on to a target cell, the takeover process begins. The host cell soon abandons its normal work, and starts to follow the virus's commands. The first thing that it does is to copy the virus's program dozens or perhaps hundreds of times. When the copies are ready, the host cell assembles new cases around them. Within as little as 20 minutes, the new viruses are complete. They are then pushed out of the cell. Unlike

THESE HUMAN IMMUNODEFICIENCY VIRUSES (HIV) ARE BREAKING AWAY FROM THEIR HOST CELL TO INFECT OTHER CELLS.

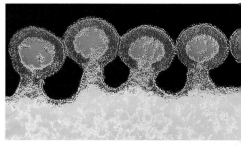

Some viruses travel in food or water, but others prefer to go by

VIRUSES ARE NOT QUITE DEAD, AND YET NOT REALLY ALIVE

insect. Yellow fever viruses, for example, travel from person to person inside mosquitoes that drink human blood. Likewise, aphids (small bugs that feed on sugary plant sap) provide a comfortable form of transport for plant viruses. To viruses, a mosquito or an aphid is like a huge passenger aircraft, with room for millions on board.

L ying in wait

Not all viruses are such keen travellers. Some sneaky types lie hidden in the body for years without doing any harm. Then, with no warning, something triggers them back to life. One of the commonest of these viruses causes the small blisters known as cold sores. Almost everyone carries this virus, but only some of us get cold sores. Exactly why is a mystery – one of the many viral puzzles that scientists are trying to solve.

APHIDS ARE BAD NEWS FOR PLANTS, BECAUSE THEY CARRY VIRUSES THAT CAUSE MANY DIFFERENT PLANT DISEASES.

WRAPPED IN A PROTECTIVE "ISOLATION
SUIT", THIS SCIENTIST IS PRACTISING THE
TECHNIQUES USED TO HANDLE DEADLY
VIRUSES IN THE LABORATORY.

Treating viruses

Despite many years of research
with snivelling volunteers,
scientists haven't yet found a
way to beat the common
cold. Many other viral
diseases have also proved
difficult to crack.

One reason for this lack
of success is that so many
viruses are involved. Colds,
for example, are caused by
more than 200 different viruses.
Another problem is that viruses
have a devious streak. Many,
including the flu virus, are able
to change the chemistry of their
outer casing. Each new chemical
"coat" works like a disguise,
throwing the body's defence
systems off the scent. To make
matters worse, viruses are not
harmed by antibiotics – drugs
that stop bacteria in their tracks.

In 1918, a lethal strain of flu
killed over 20 million people
worldwide, which is about as
many as died in World War I.
Today, more than 40 million
people are infected by the
Human Immunodeficiency
Virus (HIV), which causes the
disease known as AIDS. The
battle against viruses still has a
long way to go, but scientists
are determined to win.

BOOM TIMES

Compared to us, microbes and mini-animals are unbelievably good at reproducing. A single bacterium can have in excess of 1,000,000,000,000,000,000,000,000 offspring in just 24 hours – that's over a hundred billion times more than the human population of Earth! This kind of speedy breeding explains why microbes are so successful, and why it's so difficult to get rid of them.

THIS TUBERCULOSIS BACTERIUM IS IN THE PROCESS OF SPLITTING TO FORM TWO NEW BACTERIA.

bacteria, it could hardly be more simple. They divide in two, and each of the halves takes up a life of its own. Since only one parent is needed, there's no hint of romance at all. If it's warm and there is plenty of food, bacteria can divide as often as every 20 minutes. As a result, they are grandparents in one

Lone parents
For humans, having babies is a long, slow process. For a start, you need to find someone to produce them with, and even when that's taken care of, months go by before the happy day arrives. But for

hour flat, and great-great-great grandparents an hour after that. By the time a whole day is up, an amazing 72 generations have gone by – something that can take us nearly 2,000 years.

A SINGLE E.COLI
BACTERIUM
PRODUCED THIS
COLONY OF 200 IN
LESS THAN 3 HOURS.

Family snaps
It's very tempting to
picture elderly bacteria
surrounded by hordes
of adoring offspring.
But if bacteria had family
photo albums, the pictures
in them would tell a different
story. For a start, the family
portraits would be incredibly
dull, because all the bacteria
would look exactly the same.
This is because each one is an
exact copy of its parent, its
parent's parent, and so on, all
the way back up the family tree.
Stranger still, a parent and its
children could never appear in
the same shot. That's because
the parents actually become
their offspring when they
divide, leaving no other traces
of their old selves behind.
   After flicking through the
album for a few
thousand

TWO HOURS LATER, THE COLONY NUMBERS
MORE THAN 2,000. THEY WILL KEEP
DIVIDING UNTIL THEIR FOOD RUNS OUT.

pages, an odd fact might strike
you. This disappearing trick
means that bacteria never
actually die of old age. As long
as they don't meet with any
unpleasant accidents, they can
keep going forever.

EACH OF THE COLONIES (RED) GROWING IN
THIS PETRI DISH WAS STARTED BY A
SINGLE BACTERIUM. THE
BACTERIA ARE FEEDING
ON AGAR JELLY.

Torn apart

Multiplying by dividing is a neat trick, but bacteria are not the only things that can carry it off. Wherever there is enough water for them to live in, amoebas do it too. Amoebas are purpose-built for doing the splits because they move by changing shape. To divide, all an amoeba has to do is to set off in opposite directions at once. As the two ends crawl away, the amoeba is slowly torn in two.

Amoebas have just a single cell, but they are much bigger and far more complicated than bacteria. So before they can do the splits and divide, they have to duplicate all the bits and pieces inside the cell that they use to stay alive. The whole process takes a few hours, but even so, it's fast enough for amoebas to reproduce at a startling rate.

AMOEBAS LITERALLY RIP THEMSELVES APART TO REPRODUCE. THE TWO NEW AMOEBAS THEN GO THEIR SEPARATE WAYS.

Staying together

If being torn in two makes you feel a little squeamish, you'll be pleased to hear that not all mini- and micro-parents behave in such a drastic way. Some stick around to look after their young, and a few, such as

HANGING UPSIDE DOWN
FROM SOME WATERWEED,
THIS HYDRA HAS A
FOUR-DAY-OLD BABY
SPROUTING FROM
ITS SIDE.

parent is left comfortably in
one piece, so it can have babies
again and again.

Playing ball

There are no nurseries or
crêches in the microworld, so it

MANY MICROBES START TO BREED WHEN THEY ARE JUST MINUTES OLD

Hydra, are very attached to
them indeed. *Hydra* live in
freshwater, and spend their
lives fastened to plants. Each
one has a ring of tentacles at
the end of a slender stalk.
When a *Hydra* feels broody, it
grows a tiny bud, and this turns
into a baby *Hydra* stuck firmly
to its side. At first, the baby
shares its parent's stomach, so it
has no problem getting food.
But once it is a few days old, it
unfastens itself and creeps
away. Unlike an amoeba, its

can be difficult for adults to
keep track of their young. But
in the murky water of ponds
and streams, a micro-plant
called *Volvox* makes quite sure
that its offspring don't sneak off.
To the naked eye, it's not much
more than a small, uninteresting
blob. Under a microscope,
Volvox is revealed as a beautiful
bubble of bright green cells.
The bubble is made of jelly,
and it has a hollow centre –
the ideal place for keeping a
baby *Volvox* out of harm's way.

TUCKED AWAY INSIDE THEIR PARENTS, BABY VOLVOX WAIT TO BE RELEASED INTO THE OUTSIDE WORLD. AFTER THEY'RE RELEASED, THE PARENTS OFTEN DIE.

Volvox swims by beating tiny hairs, and each adult can have several young tumbling around inside it. But things don't stop there, as young *Volvox* can also have babies inside their own bodies, creating a collection of micro-plants that roll around like swimming Russian dolls.

F rom boom to bust

If microlife kept breeding at full speed, even for a week, the rest of us wouldn't have much fun. For a start, you could forget going out, because as soon as you set foot outside, you'd be squashed flat by a blanket of microbes reaching most of the way to the Moon.

Luckily, the microworld's boom times never last for long, because something always spoils the fun. Food and space start to run out, or even worse things happen, such as being given a good scrub, or being popped in the dishwasher aboard a dirty plate. Faced with this kind of treatment, the boom soon starts to go downhill. But microbes and mini-animals have an emergency survival trick – when times are hard, many of them produce spores or eggs. As soon as things improve, they quickly hatch out, and the boom times can begin again.

sunny day. In fact, drying out actually helps some freshwater microlife to spread. In ponds, mini-animals often scatter their eggs on the bottom, where they sink into the mud. When a pond dries out, the mud turns to dust, and the eggs are blown away by the wind. With a bit of luck, this airborne journey can end in a brand new home.

THIS TINY POND ANIMAL, CALLED A CYCLOPS, IS A FEMALE CARRYING TWO EGG PACKAGES, ONE ON EACH SIDE OF HER ABDOMEN.

Surviving hard times

Some spores can survive in boiling water for several hours, so a quick spin in the dishwasher simply gives them a good clean. Amoebas can survive for months in dried up soil, and even *Volvox* can cope if its home evaporates on a

EGG SAC

43

TINY TRAVELLERS

Swimming along at full speed, some bacteria can cover 50 times their own length every second, which is equivalent to a human moving at over 300 kmh (186 mph). Swimming is just one of the ways in which microlife gets about in a world jostling with living things. For some micro-travellers, crossing a pinhead is a major excursion. Others go on journeys that spread them far and wide.

In the swim

When you're a thousand times smaller than a full stop, going for a swim is hardly relaxing. Because you're so tiny, you weigh practically nothing, so it takes no time at all to hit top speed. But the moment you rest, you don't drift to a halt but stop dead, as if you've hit a brick wall. Even cruising is a struggle, because the water feels as thick as syrup. To make matters worse, you are repeatedly knocked off course by collisions with tiny particles. Then there's the tricky matter of the other bugs and beasts, most of which dwarf you. When they hurtle past, you're left swirling in their wake. But you don't give up, because there are no quitters in the microworld!

PARAMECIUM USES ITS "FUR COAT" TO SCOOT AROUND IN PONDS AND PUDDLES SEARCHING FOR FOOD.

GIARDIA IS A PROTIST THAT MOVES BY BEATING A SET OF EIGHT HAIRS. IT SWIMS AROUND INSIDE HUMAN INTESTINES.

MOST MICROBES HAVE ONLY TWO SPEEDS – STOP AND GO

Hairy journeys

Instead of splashing out with arms or legs, most micro-swimmers move through water by waving their hairs around. Some, such as the protists *Giardia* and *Euglena*, have long hairs called flagella. Others, including *Paramecium*, another protist, have short hairs, called cilia. *Paramecium* has a "fur coat" of cilia, which works like an all-over set of oars.

This micro-hunter zips along at 1.5 cm (0.6 in) a minute – about one-sixth the speed of a snail. It may not seem fast to us, but it would win *Paramecium* a medal at the Microlife Olympics.

Despite its speed, *Paramecium* isn't so hot at steering. To "navigate", it zooms along until it hits something solid, and then instantly goes into reverse. Rather than backing right away, like any sensible driver, it just lurches forwards again. After several

45

spin around, revolving so quickly that they become a blur. Each hair is powered by its own microscopic turbine – the only rotating motor known in the living world. When all its turbines are spinning in one direction, a bacterium's hairs bundle together and work like a

BODY STRETCHES THEN CONTRACTS.

more crashes, and more reversing, it zigzags its way clear. Being microscopic, *Paramecium* can emerge from these crunches without a scratch.

boat's propeller. But if it meets something it doesn't like, such as a whiff of bleach, it throws its turbines into reverse. This makes the hairs untangle, and the bacterium seems to tumble out of control. This is the only way it can change course because, unlike boats, bacteria don't have rudders to help them steer.

Power plants

Compared to some bacteria, *Paramecium* looks as though it's recently been to the barber's for a trim. Many bacteria have swimming hairs, or flagella, that are longer than themselves. Instead of flicking backwards and forwards, these hairs

Magnetic attraction

As well as scooting away from trouble, bacteria make a bee-line for anywhere that holds the promise of food. But how do they know which way to go, and how do they manage to stay on course? The answer, for

LOG ON...
Investigate microbe
mysteries at www.microbe.org

magnetic bacteria, is that they have a compass on board. Magnetic bacteria live in mud and need to burrow downwards to find the gloopy conditions they like. They're too small to sense the pull of gravity, so they use the Earth's magnetism. Each bacterium contains a row of iron specks,

THE PROTIST EUGLENA SWIMS TAIL-FIRST, BUT IT CAN ALSO CRAWL FORWARDS BY CHANGING ITS SHAPE — AS IT IS DOING HERE.

which pull it into line so that it's pointing from north to south. The bacterium sets off in a straight line, and because the Earth's magnetic field usually slopes downwards, it is steered safely into the mud.

THE SIX BLACK BLOBS IN THIS PICTURE ARE TINY SPECKS OF IRON THAT THIS MAGNETIC BACTERIUM USES FOR FINDING ITS WAY.

The shape changers

In the microworld, size isn't everything, and the big guys aren't necessarily the fastest. That's certainly true with amoebas, which are among the biggest and slowest microbes of all. When they are in a hurry, the best they can manage is a sluggish 2 cm (0.8 in) an hour.

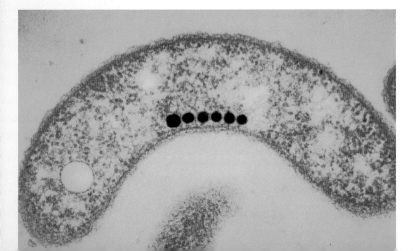

IN A SLOW-MOTION
CHASE, AN AMOEBA
REACHES FORWARDS
TO ENGULF ITS
MICROSCOPIC PREY.

"FINGERS"
REACH OUT TO
SURROUND
VICTIM.

PREY

Compared to them, *Paramecium* – at more than forty times faster – is like a Formula One racer overtaking a heavy truck. But amoebas have a good excuse for being in the microworld's slow lane. They are built like shapeless bags of jelly, and instead of using oars or propellers, they flow.

Pouring forth
To set off, an amoeba makes some of its jelly extra runny, so that it pours forwards in finger-like blobs. The "fingers" then turn solid, while the rest of the amoeba slowly catches up. By the time it's done this, another set of fingers have formed, and so millimetre by millimetre, the amoeba continues on its way. This manoeuvre is like a cross between crawling and swimming and is ideal for squeezing through narrow spaces, such as the gaps between grains of mud or sand.

These shape-changers also have "fingers" that can feel for food. If an amoeba comes into contact with a likely meal, it surrounds it and takes it on board. The victim is sealed in a bubble-like prison, where the amoeba's digestive juices slowly but surely break it down.

WEIRD WORLD
BECAUSE MICROBES AND MINI-ANIMALS ARE SO LIGHT, TAKING A TUMBLE IS NOT A PROBLEM. THE WORLD'S SMALLEST SPIDER COULD FALL FROM THE TOP OF THE EIFFEL TOWER AND THEN RUN AWAY UNHARMED.

Getting together

Amoebas are natural loners, and they usually do their best to steer clear of their own kind. But slime mould amoebas are exactly the opposite – they get together on a massive scale.

into a tiny "mushroom" that scatters thousands of spores. When the spores land, each one hatches into a new amoeba, and the bizarre cycle begins again. Slime mould "slugs" are usually pinhead size, although some

Their gatherings are the social event of a lifetime, and up to 250,000 turn up to enjoy the fun. The amoebas converge in a slimy mass, making a slug-like object that sets off across the ground. After several hours, the slug comes to a halt, and turns

can be nearly 50 cm (20 in) across. People occasionally mistake these wobbling wonders for alien life, but could creatures from outer space really be more weird than a slime mould slug?

THIS SLIME MOULD "SLUG" IS WOBBLING ITS WAY SLOWLY ACROSS THE GROUND.

Micro-hitchers

Why go to all the trouble of moving when something else can do the work for you? That's the laid-back approach taken by a gang of hangers-on from all branches of the microworld. The tiniest of these easy riders simply glue themselves on to their "ride". Bigger creatures, including most mini-animals, cling on instead. Some grip with their jaws or their feet, but soil animals called pseudoscorpions hold on with their front claws. For them, insects and spiders make ideal rides. When their ride comes to a halt, they just open their claws and drop off.

THIS PSEUDOSCORPION IS ENJOYING A FREE FLIGHT, COURTESY OF A PASSING FLY.

Doing the dung thing

Worms don't have anything to grip with, which is a problem if they're trying to catch a ride. But the microscopic worms that live in cow pats have that well under control. They stand on end like tiny threads, with their bodies waving in the air. When an insect comes to feed on the cow pat, the worms wrap themselves around its legs. Next stop – if things work out – is another tasty cow pat, just waiting to be explored.

Inner travellers

Those that aren't hangers-on sometimes travel inside their couriers. This way of travelling is used by tiny algae that live inside a type of flatworm found

SEED SHRIMPS SWIM BY
OPENING UP THEIR SHELLS
AND KICKING THEIR
FEATHERY LEGS.

on muddy beaches. Algae need sunlight to survive, which they use to make sugary food. So what's the use of being hidden inside a flatworm? Well, a flatworm's body is transparent, so light can reach the algae inside it. For the algae, it's like living in a mobile greenhouse!

The flatworm crawls out of the mud at low tide to lie in the Sun. As the tide starts to turn, it risks being swept away by the waves, so it wriggles back into the mud, hauling its passengers out of danger. In return for a safe home and trips up to the surface, the algae give some of their sugar to their kind host.

E mergency escapes

If you're caught out in the open, it's difficult to hide, even if you are smaller than a grain of sand. That's why many kinds of microlife have escape tactics that buy them time if they are attacked. Flatworms react by burrowing, while tiny seed shrimps shut themselves up in their shells, in the hope that their enemies will move on. *Paramecium* fires off sticky threads, which keep other micro-predators at bay. With so many big movers about, fast reactions are the key to survival – unless you want to end up as something else's meal.

51

AIRBORNE INVADERS

Take a deep breath, because you're about to encounter microlife that can really get up your nose. They're musty, they're mouldy, and they spread by floating through the air. They live practically everywhere, but they often go unnoticed, because they spend most of their lives hidden away. So what are they? Take a sniff – that mouldy smell is a clue…

Creepy feeders
The answer is that they're fungi. Large fungi sometimes look like plants, because they grow mushrooms and toadstools that pop up out of the ground. But unlike plants, fungi don't have roots or leaves, and they don't

need light – which is why fungi are perfectly at home in dark places, such as the back of the fridge or the inside of your trainers. You rarely see them, because most fungi live inside their food as a network of branching threads called hyphae. Fungi spread by scattering spores, which are like seeds, but too small to see. The moment a spore lands on something tasty, it comes to life and starts to grow. Within a few hours, the spore produces a mass of spreading, microscopic threads that release chemicals called enzymes to break down the food. These chemicals give the air a mouldy aroma – a sure sign that a fungus is at work.

Puff daddies

Mushrooms and toadstools are factories for making spores, just like flowers are factories for making seeds. Even small ones turn out spores on an impressive scale. The biggest, called giant puffballs, are the most prolific spore-makers on Earth. They

sprout in grassy places, and they can grow so big that you wouldn't be able to get your arms around their "waists". These fungal monsters don't qualify as microlife, but their spores certainly do. They produce up to 20,000 billion of them each – lined up side by side, that's enough to circle the world more than a dozen times.

When a puffball is ripe, it dries out and splits apart, and puffs its spores into the air like a cloud of dust. Because spores are so small, they need a lot of luck to survive. Hardly any of the spores turn into puffballs themselves – which is just as well, otherwise these flabby fungi would smother the Earth.

Freaky food

Compared to people, fungi have amazingly varied appetites. They love many of our own

THE SPORES FROM THESE PUFFBALLS ARE SO TINY THAT THEY CAN DRIFT FOR HUNDREDS OF KILOMETRES

53

favourite foods – especially if they've been left lying around for ages – but they also tuck into some weird stuff.

Some have a soft spot for wallpaper paste, glue, or leather, while one particularly fussy fungus lives on pigeon droppings (for this very choosy fungus, no other droppings will do). Another fungus lives in aircraft fuel tanks, where it dines on kerosene, and one feeds on the chemical coating you find on camera lenses – probably the flattest and thinnest meal in the world!

Mushy menus

Many fungi are vegetarians, but fresh food is something that many of them avoid. Instead, these fungi go for things that are long past their "eat by" date, such as fallen leaves or fruit. One of the smallest fungi of all – yeast – lives on the surface of fruit, where it feeds on the sugars that ooze through the fruit's skin. There's enough room for millions of yeasts on a single grape, and they make a waxy layer that you can scrape away with your thumb.

Breaking and entering

It's bad enough finding something furry in the fruit bowl, but at least you can throw mouldy food away. Things aren't quite so simple when a fungus takes over your entire home! The intruder in question is called dry rot, and it's one of the most destructive fungi in the world.

Dry rot feeds on dead wood. Its spores drift inside through open windows and doors. If they land on damp timber, they quickly set up home. Once the fungus is growing, it starts to feed hungrily, and digests wood so thoroughly that it can cause timbers to collapse. Unlike most fungi, dry rot produces extra-thick threads that can extend for several metres, which means that it can attack every single bit of timber in

WHEN DRY ROT GETS THIS BAD, IT'S TIME TO MOVE OUT, BECAUSE FLOORS CAN SUDDENLY GIVE WAY UNDERFOOT.

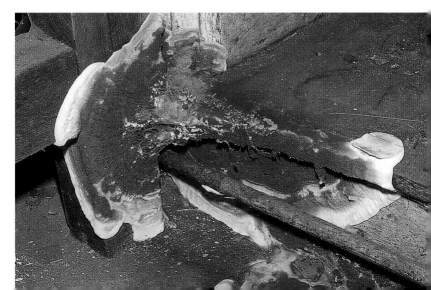

your home…and also in your neighbour's house. In the past, this formidable feeder dismantled castles and sank wooden ships. Despite careful searching, scientists have rarely found it growing in the wild.

that actually need microscopic fungi in order to stay healthy.

Underground partners
These friendly fungi live underground, where they link up with a tree's roots. The

GIANT PUFFBALLS CAN MEASURE UP TO 64 CM (25 IN) ACROSS

Eaten alive
Fungi can also threaten living wood as well. If a spore lands on a tree, it can turn into a creeping killer, which slowly devours the tree from the inside. You can tell things are bad if you see toadstools bursting out of a tree's bark. By the time this happens, the unfortunate victim is already dying. But not all woodland fungi are villains. Strangely enough, there are many trees

fungus helps the tree to collect substances from the soil, and in return the tree gives the fungus some sugary food. This cosy partnership explains why some toadstools always sprout near particular kinds of trees. For example, the fly agaric fungus teams up with silver birches. This is why you often find its red-and-white toadstools clustered in their shade. But never be tempted to touch or take a bite – these fairytale fungi

FLY AGARIC FUNGI CAN BE HARMFUL TO HUMANS, BUT THEY HELP THE TREES THAT THEY LIVE WITH TO STAY IN GOOD SHAPE.

THESE FLIES HAVE ALL BEEN KILLED BY A
PARASITIC FUNGUS, WHICH HAS DIGESTED
THEIR INTERNAL ORGANS.

are great to look
at, but they can
make you very sick.

The flycatchers

Some micro-fungi
attack living animals.
If you find a fly stuck to a
window, the chances are that
a gruesome fungus has been at
work. Called *Entomophthora*,
this fungus spreads right
through the living fly's body,
and eventually covers it in
a fluffy mould. Once
the fly is dead, the
mould unleashes a
blizzard of sticky
spores, which
fasten themselves
to anything that
comes near, such
as other flies. Soon, these
flies also become casualties.

Fortunately, very
few of these animal-
eating fungi do us
much harm. One of
the most common fungi
in humans lives between
people's toes, and causes
an irritating rash called
athlete's foot. But you
don't have to be an athlete
to catch it – all you need
is tight-fitting footwear
and sweaty feet!

UNWELCOME GUESTS

This is the chapter where things start to get personal, so if you're feeling a bit squeamish, you might want to read it later. We've already looked at some of the bacteria and viruses that the human body attracts – now it's time to check out some other mini-stowaways that can use you as their home. Some are harmless, but there are a few nasty characters that you'd probably rather avoid.

Getting a grip

Next time someone tells you something is lousy, try telling them what that really means. "Lousy" means "swarming with lice", which is probably not what they have in mind. Head lice are tiny insects that live in human hair, rather like monkeys live in the jungle. But instead of leaping around, they hang on tightly with their claws. When they feel hungry, they simply shuffle down to the scalp, bite through the skin, and slurp up the blood.

FOR THEIR SIZE, HEAD LICE HAVE AN INCREDIBLY STRONG GRIP, THANKS TO THEIR STRONG, CURVED CLAWS.

at the base of your eyelashes are some of the tiniest, measuring as little as 0.2 mm (0.008 in) long. They're called eyelash mites, and you – together with almost everybody else in the world – have probably had them since you were a few weeks old. They are tiny relatives of spiders, with sausage-shaped bodies and eight stubbly legs.

HERE, FOUR EYELASH MITES PROTRUDE FROM A FOLLICLE (A HOLE WHERE HAIR GROWS OUT OF THE SKIN).

Head lice fasten their eggs to hairs with an ultra-tough glue that makes them almost impossible to dislodge. Adult head lice sometimes rove around, and can easily spread from person to person when heads touch. They do little harm, and are quickly dealt with by a dose of special shampoo.

Micro-mites

Head lice are visible with the naked eye, but some much smaller critters also have a liking for human hair. Lurking

They live head-down next to eyelash roots, feasting on a luscious diet of dead skin cells and oily skin secretions. Because they are hidden away, few of us ever realize that they're there.

Courting couples

But here's the unpleasant part. When you're asleep, the male mites often emerge from their cosy homes with romance in mind. When a male finds a female, he mates with her on the surface of your eyelid, and a few days later she lays a batch of eggs. The adult mites often live for less than a month, but their night-time activities mean that there are always plenty of babies.

The burrowers

Eyelash mites can make your eyelids tickly, but apart from that they cause few problems. The same isn't true of another mite – one that tunnels just beneath the surface of people's skin. Called the scabies mite, it's bigger than its eyelash-dwelling relatives, and the females can excavate burrows up to 2 cm (0.8 in) long. They lay their eggs in their burrows, and once the eggs hatch, the young mites crawl out. Scabies mites make people's skin very itchy,

SCABIES MITES FEED ON LIVING SKIN, AND ARE VERY FOND OF ARMPITS AND WRISTS.

A SINGLE FLAKE OF DEAD SKIN MAKES A FILLING MEAL FOR A DUST MITE.

THE AVERAGE SINGLE BED IS HOME TO ABOUT 1 MILLION DUST MITES

and they are spread easily by skin contact. Luckily, outbreaks are rare, so your chances of catching them are low.

Dining on dust

The last member of this mitey trio doesn't live on the body itself. Instead, it feeds on bits of dandruff and other flakes of old dead skin. Your body sheds these flakes all the time, and they gather in corners and crevices, and also in bedding – places where the dust mite likes to hang out. This microscopic scavenger grips skin flakes in its tiny pincers and slowly sucks up the appetizing nutrients that they contain. Yum!

Dust mites don't do any harm themselves, but they can cause trouble. That's because their droppings often swirl about in household air, where people can breathe them in. These drifting droppings can trigger off asthma – what better reason for tackling the dust that's building up in your bedroom!

Airborne arrivals
There's nothing more annoying than being kept awake by mosquitoes, but itchy bites aren't the only problems that they cause. In some parts of the world, mosquitoes carry some really vile microlife, which they pass on when they prick your skin to drink your blood. One of these rogues is the parasite that causes malaria – a dangerous disease affecting up to 200 million people a year.

Malaria
The malaria parasite is a protist (a single-celled creature). It's so small that it can fit inside your own body's cells – even the tiny red ones that circulate in your blood. If you're unlucky enough to catch it, that's one of the places where it feeds, and also where it multiplies. At night, malaria parasites break out of their red blood cell hideaways and move into the liquid part of the blood. It's cunning timing, because that's when hungry mosquitoes are on the move. If another mosquito bites you, it picks up some of the parasites and hands them on to someone else.

A SINGLE MOSQUITO BITE CAN INJECT THOUSANDS OF PARASITES INTO A PERSON'S BLOOD.

A "MOZZY NET" IS A GOOD WAY OF KEEPING MOSQUITOES AT BAY WHILE YOU SLEEP.

Malaria can be fatal if it's not treated in time. But it doesn't just affect humans – it's also a threat to many wild animals, from apes and monkeys to lizards and birds.

All aboard

Malaria mosquitoes live mainly in the tropics, where it's warm all year round. So do some other insects that harbour nasty microlife in their bodies. In Africa, the tsetse fly spreads the parasite that causes sleeping sickness, which results in fever, extreme tiredness, and even brain damage. In South America, the creepily named assassin bug is almost as bad, spreading a parasite that affects the body in a similar way. You can also get parasites from contaminated water, which is how an amoeba that causes dysentery gets into the body. In fact, you are so attractive to microlife that unwelcome guests can't wait to get aboard!

THIS AMOEBA CAUSES DYSENTERY, A DISEASE THAT INVOLVES SEVERE DIARRHOEA AND INTESTINAL PAIN.

63

LIFE BELOW GROUND

I f you want to get to grips with microlife, there's no better way than to put on some gardening gloves and scoop up a handful of soil. Besides earthworms and beetles, it will contain hundreds of mini-animals, millions of microscopic fungi, and billions of bacteria. Soil is like an underground larder, because it's packed with living things and rotting remains that microlife can use as food.

GRASS

TOP-SOIL

SUB-SOIL

ROCK PIECES

SOLID ROCK

Hunters below ground

Life in the soil may be dark, but for its micro-inhabitants, it's certainly not dull. This subterranean world teems with predators, and few of them are more common – or more deadly – than pseudoscorpions. Their name is a bit of a mouthful, but it makes sense when you know that "pseudo" just means "fake" or "phoney". Unlike the real thing, these scorpion-lookalikes are only a few millimetres long, and they don't have stings or tails. But they do have fearsome weapons – two pincers that can inject lethal poison into prey.

THIS MODEL SHOWS A SLICE THROUGH THE SOIL. MOST SOIL MICROBES LIVE NEAR THE SURFACE IN THE TOP-SOIL, WHERE THERE ARE LOTS OF DEAD REMAINS TO EAT.

A PSEUDOSCORPION'S PINCERS CONTAIN GLANDS THAT MAKE POISON AND OTHERS THAT PRODUCE SILK.

for example, they politely "shake pincers". The pincers also produce silk, which the pseudoscorpions use to make a protective wrapping for their eggs. Finally, if pseudoscorpions fancy a change of scenery, they simply climb to the surface and grab a lift on bigger animals passing by.

Pincer power

Pseudoscorpions are far too small to puncture human skin with their pincers, so they won't do you any harm. But for other mini-animals in the soil, such as springtails or proturans, these poison-packed predators are killers. Pseudoscorpions track down their food using their highly developed sense of touch. The moment they feel something edible, the pincers snap shut around their victims.

Their pincers also come in handy in other ways. When pseudoscorpions meet,

Micro-worms

Compared to pseudoscorpions, earthworms are monster-size, and definitely don't qualify as microlife. But in the soil, there are lots of other worms, and over 99.999 per cent of them are invisible to the naked eye.

PROTURANS ARE BLIND, WINGLESS INSECTS THAT FEEL THEIR WAY THROUGH THE SOIL WITH THEIR LARGE FRONT LEGS.

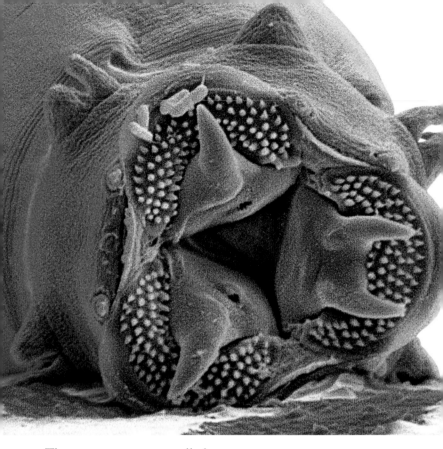

The commonest type, called roundworms, have cylindrical bodies. Roundworms are often small enough to live in the tiny spaces between specks of soil.

THIS ROUNDWORM'S MOUTH HAS THREE LIPS AND THREE FORKED "TEETH" THAT RASP AWAY AT ITS FOOD.

Deadly snares

Most roundworms aren't strong enough to tunnel, so instead they wriggle their way through the soil. If they sense danger ahead, they go into reverse and wriggle their way out of trouble. This escape strategy usually works, but not when a worm blunders head-first into one of the world's smallest, strangest traps. These traps are shaped like triangular nooses, and they are grown by a fungus that has a taste for animal prey. When a worm wriggles into a trap, the noose suddenly swells up to ensnare the worm. No matter how hard it struggles, it can't get free. Once the worm is dead, the fungus grows into it, and digests its body from the inside.

The decomposers

You'll be glad to hear that these merciless hunters are heavily outnumbered below ground. In fact, most of the soil's inhabitants are harmless microbes that feed on dead remains. Called decomposers, they are nature's recyclers. They break down anything that was once alive, so that its nutrients can be used again. The warmer the soil, the faster the decomposers work. That's why dead leaves often last all winter, but disappear in spring as the weather gets warmer.

Compost cookers

When these recyclers are really busy, they actually produce heat themselves. And when they are crowded together – such as in a compost heap – the temperature can really start to climb. In a small compost heap, the temperature inside often reaches 40°C (104°F), which is warmer than the inside of a human body. In a big heap, it can be up to 70°C (158°F) – that's hot enough to slowly cook an egg (although it's perhaps not the most hygienic place to prepare breakfast). Farmers have to be particularly careful about these heat-producing microbes, because they can sometimes make haystacks catch fire.

Protect your grub

Food is precious to all microbes, and there's nothing worse than having to share a meal. Soil

A TECHNICIAN CHECKS THE TEMPERATURE INSIDE A COMPOST HEAP AT A RECYCLING CENTRE. A HIGH TEMPERATURE SHOWS THAT BACTERIA ARE BUSY AT WORK.

LOG ON...
www.microbeworld.org/
mlc/pages/activities.asp

WEIRD WORLD

ROUNDWORMS GATHER IN LARGE NUMBERS WHERE THERE'S PLENTY OF FOOD. THERE CAN BE 100,000 IN A SINGLE FALLEN APPLE, AND OVER 500,000 IN A PATCH OF SOIL THE SIZE OF THIS BOOK.

microbes don't have teeth to scare off would-be food thieves, or sharp elbows to shove them aside. But they do have some sneaky ways of keeping food to themselves. One trick is to multiply really quickly, so that anything nearby gets swamped by the sheer numbers of microbes. Another tactic is to

but a fungus had landed on it and had started to grow. Normally, the plate would have gone straight in the bin, but the researcher noticed that the fungus was surrounded by an empty space. The

SCOTSMAN ALEXANDER FLEMING DISCOVERED PENICILLIN – A NATURAL DRUG THAT HAS SAVED MILLIONS OF LIVES.

release chemicals that repel any raiders trying to grab their grub.

Antibiotics
Scientists stumbled across this chemical warfare quite by accident when a researcher spotted something weird on a laboratory plate. The plate was

fungus had created this "no-go zone" by producing a chemical that was deadly to the bacteria. The date was 1928, and the researcher – Alexander Fleming – had discovered penicillin, the world's first-known antibiotic.

Microbes at war
Antibiotics have proved to be incredibly valuable to humans, because they kill many of the bacteria that cause disease. But

deadly nerve poison. Tetanus bacteria get into the body through deep cuts, the kind made by rusty blades and nails buried in the soil. Once inside, its poison makes all the body's muscles seize up, which means that the unlucky victim cannot breathe. At one time, tetanus claimed many lives, but today you can be protected from it for years by a single injection.

the fungi and other microbes that make them in the first place. Wherever there is food to be eaten, these recyclers use antibiotics to keep competitors under control. In this micro-warfare, the "battlegrounds" can be smaller than a full stop, as neighbouring microbes struggle to defend their territory.

Poisonous to people

Although we're not part of these hostilities, the soil does contain microbes that can do us serious harm. One of the nastiest is the tetanus bacterium – a germ that can release a

THE TETANUS
BACTERIUM
DOESN'T LIKE
OXYGEN, WHICH
EXPLAINS WHY IT IS
NORMALLY FOUND
UNDERGROUND.

69

GOING TO EXTREMES

How would you feel after being bombarded by X-rays, cooked in near-boiling water, or trapped underground with no chance of escape? The answer is not too good! But for some bacteria and micro-animals, called "extremophiles", such conditions pose no problems. They love going to extremes, and their amazing toughness lets them thrive in places where few other things can live.

Chilling out

You don't have to look far to find extremophiles. The chances are that you have a few tucking into the food in your fridge, where the temperature is about 4°C (39°F). Many microbes grind to a halt when it's this cold, but some bacteria and fungi take it in their stride. That's why food left in the fridge eventually goes "off".

Life is tougher in a freezer, because it's a finger-numbing −18°C (0°F), which is way too cold for microbes to grow. But they're still in there, and when

ANTARCTICA'S DRY VALLEYS ARE AMONG THE HARSHEST PLACES ON EARTH, BUT MICROBES STILL MANAGE TO SURVIVE HERE.

THIS BANK OF SNOW HAS BEEN TURNED RED BY A MASS OF MICROSCOPIC ALGAE.

food defrosts, they wake up and get back to work.

Dry-valley dwellers

A favourite place for cold-proof microbes is at the bottom of the oceans, where the water is fridge-like all year round. Cold-proof bugs also live in polar ice, but some of the hardiest live in Antarctica's dry valleys, where no snow has fallen for more than a million years. Temperatures in winter can drop to –50°C (–58°F). Even in summer, it rarely gets above freezing point – that's hardly a heatwave, but it's enough to bring the valleys' microbes to life. Polar microbes live just under the surface of rocks and survive by taking energy from sunshine. In other parts of the world, similar microbes live in drifts of mountain snow. They can turn the snow red or orange, giving passing skiers a real surprise.

Absolute what?

In Antarctica, the coldest temperature ever recorded was −89°C (−128°F). But in the lab, scientists can cool things down to near −273°C (−459°F). This temperature is called absolute

Taking the plunge

So what happens when microlife really catches cold? The answer is an amazing one – it sometimes survives.

ALTHOUGH THEY ARE BARELY VISIBLE TO THE NAKED EYE, TARDIGRADES ARE PROBABLY THE TOUGHEST ANIMALS ON EARTH.

zero, and it is the coldest that anything can get. Scientists haven't managed to produce this rock-bottom temperature yet, but they've come close to it. Rather than braving it for themselves, they have tried it out on microlife.

Bacteria often pull through unharmed, but more incredibly, some micro-animals do as well. The real experts are eight-legged tardigrades, also known as water bears. They are outstanding survivors – not only through the bitterest cold, but also through droughts that can last for years.

Freeze-dried life

Tardigrades are water animals, although strangely they cannot swim. They live in gutters, puddles, and tree-holes, and all sorts of other places that often dry up. When the water starts to disappear, they activate the "Tardigrade Survival Plan".

They tuck in their legs, turn into barrel-shaped blobs, and start to dry up as well. For most animals, this would be madness, but tardigrades do their drying in a carefully controlled way. Soon, their water content drops to about 2 per cent – that's even less than in a potato crisp. Once they are dehydrated, they contain so little water that they are not damaged by ice crystals if they freeze. Tucked up, dried out, and deep frozen, they can survive for a decade or more.

Feeling the heat

Up at the other end of the thermometer, heat can be a real problem for microlife. When the temperature reaches 50°C

LOG ON...
http://commtechlab.msu.edu/sites/dlc-me/zoo/index.html

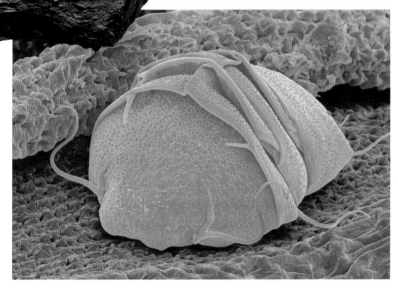

WITH ITS LEGS TUCKED IN, THIS DRIED-OUT TARDIGRADE CAN SURVIVE CONDITIONS THAT WOULD KILL MOST LIVING THINGS.

FOR HUMANS, A DIP IN THIS HOT SPRING WOULD BE FATAL, BUT HEAT-LOVING BACTERIA SPEND THEIR WHOLE LIVES IN THE SHALLOWS AROUND ITS RIM.

(122°F), most microbes and mini-animals start to feel out of sorts. By the time it hits 60°C (140°F), many are dead. Heat cooks their essential chemicals so that they cannot function. But heat-loving microbes, or "thermophiles", are specially adapted to withstand high temperatures, and some survive in surroundings that are too hot for us to touch.

Bubble trouble

In America's Yellowstone National Park, heat-loving microlife is really at home. Here, scalding-hot water bubbles up through the Earth's crust, creating pools that give off clouds of steam. Many of the pools register 70°C (158°F), and a few reach a seriously hot 85°C (185°F). Water as warm as this is off-limits to all animal life, because anything that swims in it would be instantly poached. But in the shallows, where things are slightly cooler, the water is full of strands of coloured slime.

You guessed – it's microlife, waving as the current flows past. These strands are formed by bacteria, and to cope with their steamy surroundings, they have "anti-cook" chemicals inside them rather than anti-freeze.

The chemical lovers

By far the most rugged microbe in Yellowstone is a heat-proof and acid-proof bacterium. It lives in pools of hot sulphuric acid that can easily burn metal or skin, but they don't seem to bother the bacterium one bit.

Acid pools are not the only habitats that resemble outdoor chemistry sets. Desert lakes in dry parts of the world may be 10 times saltier than the sea. So if you took away all their water and left the salt behind, they would still be more than one-third full. But even here, certain salt-loving microbes manage to thrive.

THESE SCALDING-HOT GEYSERS HAVE BUILT UP MOUNDS OF MINERAL-RICH ROCK – ANOTHER IDEAL HOME FOR HEAT-LOVING MICROBES.

Black smokers

In 1977, a team of scientists
stumbled across the Earth's
most extreme habitat. More
than 2.5 km (1.5 miles) down on
the floor of the Pacific Ocean,
they found rocky cracks and
chimneys, or "vents", billowing
jet-black water into the sea. As
their submersible approached
one of these "black smokers",
its temperature gauge started to
melt. They backed away, which
was just as well, because these
deep-sea vents can reach 350°C
(662°F). Nothing can live in
water as hot as this, but microlife
gets very close.

Record breaker

Around each smoker is a wafer-
thin zone of cooler water,
where the temperature is
midway between superhot and
icy cold. This is the home of
the world's most heat-resistant
bacteria, which can survive at a
record-breaking 113°C (235°F).
Because the water pressure at
this depth is immense, it
prevents the water from boiling
– which would destroy the
bacteria's home.

Life in rock

If you find this strange lifestyle
difficult to imagine, here's one
that's even odder. Engineers
drilling for oil have discovered
bacteria nearly 3 km (2 miles)
below ground. Like the vent-
dwellers, these bacteria can
cope with extreme heat and
pressure, but they also have to
put up with the world's most
claustrophobic surroundings.
Their homes are water-filled
cracks in solid rock. Down in
these dark, tiny prisons,
nothing happens for
centuries on end, and no
visitors ever call.

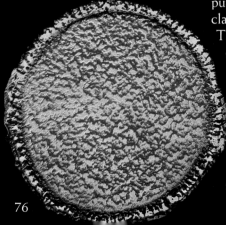

STAPHYLOTHERMUS IS ONE OF
THE BACTERIA THAT ARE FOUND
AROUND BLACK SMOKERS ON THE
DEEP OCEAN FLOOR.

BLACK SMOKERS ARE
PLACES WHERE
MINERAL-RICH WATER
GUSHES OUT FROM DEEP
INSIDE THE EARTH.

No one knows exactly how far bacteria reach underground. For subterranean bugs, heat is the biggest headache, because the deeper they go, the hotter it gets. Under dry land, things get too hot for life at depths of about 4 km (2.5 miles). But under the oceans, rocks heat up more slowly, so here buried bacteria may live deeper still.

Sole survivors

On the Earth's surface, most bacteria feed on living things or dead remains. But bacteria that dwell several kilometres underground find that the food cupboard is practically bare, because there is almost no other life at these depths. Instead, buried bugs survive by eating the Earth itself! They collect minerals that dissolve in underground water, and use them to produce chemical reactions that give the bacteria energy. It's a strange way of life, but an ancient one.

If the Sun died tomorrow, plants would stop growing. Soon after that, life on the Earth's surface would stop. But deep underground, and around deep-sea vents, these primitive, mineral-munching bugs would carry on just as before.

Back from the past

Whether they are poisoned or starved, chilled or grilled, bacteria still manage to keep on going. But microbes are even tougher when they

SCIENTISTS THINK IT'S POSSIBLE THAT THERE MAY BE BACTERIA LIVING UNDER THE ROCKY SURFACE OF MARS.

turn into spores, which can stay alive for astounding lengths of time. Scientists have revived spores from inside a prehistoric bee found in amber (fossilized tree sap). When that bee was buzzing around, 40 million years ago, giant flightless birds roamed the Earth. After the spores were "woken up", they produced normal bacteria, just

have found them as high up as 40 km (25 miles). So if bacteria can stay alive in the atmosphere, could they survive in the most challenging habitat of all – space? To try to answer this question, scientists have exposed bacteria to space-like conditions in the lab. They have blasted them with X-rays, kept them in a vacuum for months, and then

like ones alive today. Another scientist claims to have revived spores from salt deposits over 250 million years old. That's before the Age of Dinosaurs!

Bugs in space
Living bacteria have been found 16 km (10 miles) up in the air, blown to that height by the wind. Some scientists claim to

IT SEEMS LIKELY THAT BACTERIA COULD SURVIVE IN SPACE, BUT WE CAN'T BE SURE.

given them a deep-deep-freeze, (in space it's much worse than icy cold). By this stage, you'll know the results. Yes, bacterial spores can put up with this cruel treatment as well. So are there bacteria in space? The truth is out there somewhere...

MICROLIFE AND US

Compared to bigger living things, microbes don't win many prizes for popularity. They're not fluffy or cuddly, they don't make good pets, and some of them can make you extremely ill. So wouldn't we be much better off if there were no microbes at all? The answer is a big, big "No!" Microbes may be a mixed bunch, but one thing's for sure – without them, we simply wouldn't exist.

Caught short

If you think that sounds a bit far-fetched, imagine waking up and discovering that all the world's microlife had suddenly disappeared. What difference would it make to your day? Initially, not much, but an hour or two after breakfast you'd start to notice some ominous rumblings down below. That's because you rely on microbes to help you digest your food. Without them, your digestive system would be in trouble, and some important nutrients would travel straight through you and out the other end.

A SANDWICH LIKE THIS MAKES A TASTY MEAL, BUT WITHOUT BACTERIA, ITS FILLING WOULD BE IMPOSSIBLE TO DIGEST.

EACH OF THESE CHEESES CONTAINS BILLIONS OF BACTERIA. IN FACT, CHEESES ARE MADE BY LETTING BACTERIA FEED ON SUBSTANCES IN MILK.

Closing time

After a few days in your new bug-free body, you would be hungry and tired, although your skin and teeth would be feeling extra-clean. But some unusual things would be happening in the world around you. For a start, all the world's bakeries and breweries would have closed, along with the processing plants that make yoghurt and cheese. These use products made by microbes, so without them, the processes just wouldn't work.

For the same reason, many pharmaceutical factories would also have shut down. And, you may be surprised to hear, so would factories that produce shiny paper, such as the page you're looking at right now. So without microlife, you'd also have to live without illustrated books and glossy magazines.

Harvests on hold

You could probably do without these things, although life wouldn't be a bundle of fun. But in the natural world, some

BREAD AND ALCOHOLIC DRINKS ARE MADE WITH THE HELP OF YEASTS – SINGLE-CELLED FUNGI THAT HAVE A TASTE FOR SUGAR.

far more threatening changes would be looming on the horizon – or underneath it. After a few days, many of the world's crop plants would be looking sickly, and within weeks, they would start to die. So too would many wild plants, including nearly all trees. That's because most plants rely on bacteria and microscopic fungi in the soil.

LONG AGO, THE ANCESTORS OF THIS CYANOBACTERIUM MADE THE AIR FIT TO BREATHE, ENABLING ANIMALS TO EVOLVE.

If there were no bacteria, there would be nothing for plant-eating animals to eat. And as a result, there'd be no food for animals that eat other animals.

That means you
To make matters worse, nothing would rot down. Dead

WE NEED MICROBES FAR MORE THAN MICROBES NEED US

COWS HAVE FOUR STOMACH CHAMBERS. THE BIGGEST OF THESE IS FILLED WITH PLANT-DIGESTING MICROBES.

vegetation would blow around the streets, piling up like drifts of snow. Dead animals would be everywhere – often dried out, but otherwise perfectly preserved. Life in the sea would also be badly hit, because without microscopic plankton, very little could survive. And once our food reserves began to run low, the human race would be on the danger list too. But luckily, none of this is going to happen. Microlife is alive and well, and most definitely here to stay.

A breath of fresh air!
So you can heave a sigh of relief. And as you do, here's a thought about

Not (quite) guilty

If microbes ever went on trial, these plus points would make a good case for the defence. However, even though we need microlife as a whole, there are some kinds that we could definitely do without. They are the ones that cause illness and disease.

the oxygen that keeps you alive. Nearly four billion years ago, when life began, the Earth's atmosphere contained no oxygen at all. But about 500 million years later, primitive organisms called cyanobacteria developed, which released oxygen into the air. Thanks to these bugs, the atmosphere's oxygen level slowly started to climb, making the air fit to breathe. Today, plants also give off oxygen, but microbes are still doing it too.

STROMATOLITES ARE ROCKY MOUNDS MADE BY CYANOBACTERIA IN SHALLOW WATER. SOME FOSSILIZED STROMATOLITES DATE BACK MORE THAN 3 BILLION YEARS.

Today, the most dangerous kinds are the microbes that cause malaria, tuberculosis, and AIDS. In the past, other major killers included smallpox and plague. These diseases often flared up without warning and swept across whole continents, leaving millions of casualties.

But there's a flip side. Thanks to microlife, we have antibiotics and vaccinations to prevent or control diseases that were once life-threatening. In fact, the smallpox virus has been totally wiped out – an amazing success in the fight against disease. Unfortunately, not all microbes are that easily beaten.

Helping hands
So remember, for every "bad guy" in the microworld there are hundreds

WEIRD WORLD
WITHOUT MICROBES, HOLIDAYS WOULD NEVER BE THE SAME AGAIN, BECAUSE THE SEASIDE WOULD LOSE ITS FAMILIAR BRINY SMELL. THAT'S BECAUSE IT'S CAUSED BY MICROBES CAUSING SEAWEED TO ROT.

of decent microbes that help us in all kinds of different ways. The next time you see someone reach for the bleach, tactfully remind them that we need microlife to survive.

A QUICK JAB WITH A SYRINGE AT THE DOCTORS IS ENOUGH TO KEEP MANY OF THE MOST DANGEROUS MICROBES AT BAY.

REFERENCE SECTION

Whether you've finished reading *Microlife*, or are turning to this section first, you'll find the information on the next eight pages really helpful. Here are all the facts and figures, background details, and unfamiliar words that will notch up your knowledge. You'll also find a list of website addresses – so, whether you want to surf the net or search out facts, these pages should turn you from an enthusiast into an expert.

MICROLIFE CLASSIFICATION

In order to discuss all the different species of living things, scientists classify them into a series of categories according to the features that they share. (The only exceptions are viruses, which are not truly alive.) In classification, the largest categories are called kingdoms. There are a total of five kingdoms, and all of them contain some species that are microscopic. Kingdoms are divided into smaller categories, which are further divided until individual species are reached. This chart shows the classification of the house dust mite.

Kingdom: Animalia
This contains more than 30 phyla of multi-celled animals.

Phylum: Arthropoda
Over 15 classes of animals with outer body cases, and often wings.

Class: Arachnida
Arachnids have four pairs of legs. There are over 75,000 species.

Order: Acari
This order contains about 35,000 species of ticks and mites.

Family: Pyroglyphididae
Over 1,000 mite species, all with short legs and long sensory hairs.

Genus: *Dermatophagoides*
About 20 similar species of dust mite that feed on flakes of skin.

Species: *Dermatophagoides farinae*
This is the house dust mite, which is almost always found indoors.

KEY MICROLIFE GROUPS

This chart describes the most important microlife groups. Some contain only microscopic species, but many contain a mixture of microscopic species and ones that can be seen with the naked eye. The totals show the numbers of species (or different types, in the case of viruses) that have been identified by scientists. In some cases, lots more species are probably awaiting discovery.

NAME	EXAMPLES	TOTAL	FEATURES
Viruses			
Animal viruses	Flu virus, common cold	Total unknown	Attack animal cells. Many cause diseases, but others do little harm.
Plant viruses	Potato mosaic virus, tulip breaking virus	Total unknown	Attack plant cells. Mosaic viruses can be as long as some bacteria.
Bacterial viruses (also known as bacteriophages)	T4 bacteriophage	About 500	Attack bacteria. They include the most complex viruses known.
Bacteria			
Archaebacteria	*Sulfolobus*	250	Ancient bacteria group. Often inhabit places such as hot springs and salt lakes.
Cyanobacteria (also known as blue-green algae)	*Anabaena*	1,700	Bacteria that live by collecting the energy in sunlight.
Mycoplasmas	*Thermoplasma*	100	Smallest bacteria. Unique, as they have no cell walls.
Enterobacteria	*E. coli*	4,000	Typically found inside the digestive systems of animals. Most are harmless, but some cause disease.
Filament-forming bacteria	*Streptomyces*	500	Bacteria that join together to form long threads. Many live in the soil.

Name	Examples	Total	Features
Nitrogen-fixing bacteria	Nitrobacter	50	Live in soil, or in growths on plant roots. They turn nitrogen into a form that plants can use.
Protists			
Amoebas and relatives	Amoeba	15,000	Animal-like protists that move by changing shape.
Ciliates	Paramecium	8,000	Animal-like protists that move by beating minute hairs called cilia.
Dinoflagellates	Ceratium	2,100	Behave like a cross between plants and animals.
Green algae	Chlorella, Volvox	7,000	Plant-like protists. Collect energy from sunshine. Many live in groups or colonies, which may resemble plants.
Diatoms	Asterionella	5,000	Plant-like protists. Protected by a silica case made of two close-fitting parts.
Fungi			
Sac fungi	Bread mould, truffle	30,000	Make spores in microscopic sacs. Many sac fungi attack plants, causing diseases.
Yeasts	Baker's yeast	500	Single-celled sac fungi. Most live on plants, but some live on body surfaces.
Club fungi	Giant puffball, fly agaric toadstool	16,000	Make spores in microscopic clubs. Includes nearly all mushrooms and toadstools.
Typical moulds	Entomophthora, pin mould	750	Includes many small and microscopic moulds, including some that attack insects and other animals.

Conidial fungi	*Penicillium*, bread mould, black mould	17,500	Do not use sexual reproduction. Many attack plants, causing diseases.
Animals			
Cnidarians	*Hydra*	9,000	Have stinging tentacles. Most live in the sea, but a few are freshwater animals.
Flatworms	Tapeworms, blood flukes	13,000	Flat-bodied worms. Some are parasites.
Roundworms	*Ditylenchus*, *Trichinella*	15,000	Body is cylindrical and not divided into segments. Many microscopic species are soil-dwellers or parasites.
Tardigrades (or water bears)	*Hypsibius*	600	Eight-legged animals that live in fresh and saltwater.
Rotifers	*Asplancha*	2,000	Legless water animals that collect food by beating a double crown of tiny hairs.
Arthropods: Crustaceans	*Cyclops*, water flea	40,000	Animals with a hard body case, sometimes armed with pincers. Most live in water.
Arthropods: Arachnids	Mites, pseudoscorpions	75,000	Hard body case and eight legs. Most live on land.
Arthropods: Proturans	*Eosentomon*	400	Hard body case and six legs. Common in soil.
Arthropods: Collembolans	*Sminthurus*	6,500	Humped bodies and a spring-like jumping device. Common in soil.
Arthropods: Diplurans	*Catajapyx*	800	Insect-like animals. Resemble earwigs. Common in soil.
Arthropods: Insects	Human head and body lice	1,000,000+	Hard body case and six legs. Many have wings. Almost all live on land

MICROLIFE RECORDS

Smallest living thing
The smallest fully living thing is a bacterium called *Mycoplasma laidlawii*, which can be just 0.0002 mm (0.000008 in) across. Many viruses are smaller than this, but they are not considered to be fully alive.

Smallest animal
Some freshwater rotifers are just 0.04 mm (0.0016 in) long, which is a lot smaller than the biggest bacteria. These tiny animals live in ponds, and in films of water on mosses and particles of soil. Despite being so minute, rotifers have bodies containing lots of cells, while bacteria have just one cell.

Simplest animal
The world's most simple animal is called *Trichoplax adhaerens*, and it is the only member of a group called the placozoans. This creature lives in the ocean, and it looks like a tiny creeping pancake. *Trichoplax adhaerens* was first discovered in 1883, on the glass of a seawater aquarium.

Biggest single-celled creature
Most single-celled creatures are microscopic, but a few can reach an impressive size. One of the biggest ever was a species called *Nummulites*, which grew up to 15 cm (6 in) across. Fossils of this giant protist can be seen in the rock that was used to build the pyramids of Ancient Egypt.

Biggest bacterium
A bacterium called *Thiomargarita namibiensis* can grow to 1 mm (0.0 4 in) in length, which means that, amazingly, it's visible to the naked eye. Discovered in 1997 off the coast of Namibia, this gigantic bacterium lives in sediment on the seabed.

Biggest virus
A virus called *Citrus tristeza*, which infects citrus fruits, is 0.02 mm (0.0008 in) long, making it the longest virus known.

Longest-lived microbe
Under normal conditions, the longest-lived microbes are probably roundworms and other parasites, which can have lifespans of more than 10 years. However, if periods of dormancy (resting) are included, the longest-lived microbes are bacteria, which can survive for thousands or millions of years.

First microbes on Earth
In Australia, microscopic fossils of bacteria have been found in rocks that are 3.5 billion years old, making them the oldest known living things on Earth. The Earth itself formed about 4.5 billion years ago.

Fastest microbe
For its size, the fastest-moving microbe is a bacterium called *Bdellovibrio bacteriovorus*. It can swim 50 times its own length in a second, which is equivalent to a human swimming at about 325 kmh (202 mph) – almost as fast as the world's fastest powerboat!

Largest mobile colonies
In the sea, some radiolarians live together in giant sausage-shaped colonies, which drift slowly through the water. The colonies look like transparent worms, and can measure up to 3 m (10 ft) long.

Deadliest bacterium

For humans, the deadliest bacterium is *Yersinia pestis*, which causes the plague. One form of the disease, bubonic plague, has a mortality rate of 50–75 per cent. Another form, pneumonic plague, is almost always fatal.

Deadliest virus

The most dangerous viruses are filoviruses. Two of them – the Ebola and Marburg viruses – cause diseases that have a mortality rate of up to 90 per cent. Filoviruses normally spread to humans from monkeys.

MICROLIFE WEBSITES

http://nationalgeographic.com/world/0010/bacteria
Get the low-down on bugs and germs from National Geographic.

www.microscopy-uk.org.uk
One of the most interesting microlife sites on the web, packed with information and pictures, and links to other microworld sites.

www.cellsalive.com/
Find out more about living cells at this site, which includes animations.

www.amnh.org/nationalcenter/infection/index.html
Visit the American Museum of Natural History's web pages on microbes to find out about the problems that some of them can cause.

www.pfizer.com/rd/microbes/index.html
Specially designed for younger users and based on a travelling exhibition, this microbe site is created by one of the world's leading pharmaceutical companies that specializes in bug-busting drugs.

www.ucmp.berkeley.edu/collections/micro.html
Created by the Museum of Paleontology at the University of California at Berkeley, this site contains images of microfossils – the fossilized remains of ancient microbes.

http://quest.arc.nasa.gov/projects/astrobiology/fieldwork/students.html
This NASA site is packed with information and projects about microbial life and space.

www.uq.edu.au/nanoworld/images_1.html
The University of Queensland's Centre for Microscopy has some fascinating images of microlife on this site.

www.denniskunkel.com/PublicHtml/EducationSplash.asp
See some amazing pictures of microscopic life at this site, published by a leading expert in the field.

www.ualberta.ca/~csotonyi/extremophiles/images/index.html
Check out this site for pictures of extremophile microbes.

www.eurekascience.com/ICanDoThat/bacteria_cells.htm
Basic bacteria info in a friendly format.

GLOSSARY

Algae (singular – alga)
Simple organisms that live like plants by collecting energy from sunlight. Many algae are microscopic, but the biggest – called seaweeds – can be dozens of metres long.

Antibiotics
Substances produced by some fungi and bacteria that kill other microbes growing nearby.

Antibodies
Chemicals made by the body's immune system to deactivate or destroy invading microbes.

Bacteriophage
A virus that attacks bacteria.

Bacteria (singular – bacterium)
Microbes that consist of a single, simple cell. Also known as germs, bacteria are the smallest and most numerous living things on Earth.

Bloom
A population explosion in water of algae or other plant-like microbes.

Budding
A form of reproduction that begins with a bud appearing on a parent organism. The bud slowly grows into a new individual.

Cells
The smallest units of living matter, which are each surrounded by a protective membrane. Most animals and plants have millions of cells, but microbes often have just one.

Cellulose
A substance that forms the cell walls of plants, algae, and some fungi.

Cilia (singular – cilium)
Tiny hair-like structures found on the surface of some microbes. Cilia can beat to make a microbe move.

Colonies
In the microworld, collections of individual microbes that live together in a group. Colonies are often big enough see without a microscope.

Cytoplasm
A jelly-like substance inside a living cell. The cytoplasm surrounds the nucleus – the cell's command centre, which contains DNA.

Decomposers
Things that feed on dead remains, and that help to break them down. Most decomposers are microbes.

DNA (deoxyribonucleic acid)
This is the chemical that carries all the information needed to build a living thing and keep it alive. DNA is passed from one generation to the next when living things reproduce.

Electron microscope
A microscope that works by using a beam of minute particles, called electrons, instead of using light.

Extremophile
Anything that lives in places that experience extreme conditions.

Flagella (singular – flagellum)
Hair-like structures, longer than cilia, that many microbes use to move. Unlike real hair, flagella can spin around, or flick from side to side.

Fungi (singular – fungus)
Living things that absorb food from living or dead matter around them. Fungi reproduce by releasing spores.

Glands
Organs that make and release chemicals, such as poisons used for killing prey.

Habitat
The surroundings and resources that any living thing needs for survival.

Host
The particular species of living thing that a parasite uses for its food, and usually as a home as well.

Immune system
In animals, a collection of physical and chemical defences that help to keep harmful microbes at bay.

Larvae (singular – larva)
Young animals that look quite different from their parents, and that live in different ways. Larvae change shape as they grow up.

Membrane
A thin covering around a cell, or around part of an animal or plant.

Microbe
Another word for a micro-organism.

Micro-organism
Any living thing that is too small to be seen without a microscope.

Organism
Anything that is alive.

Parasite
Something that lives on or inside another species, which is called its host. Parasites are usually much smaller than their hosts.

Pathogen
Any microbe that causes a disease.

Phytoplankton
Free-floating algae and other plant-like organisms in the ocean. They live by collecting the energy in sunlight.

Plankton
A mass of small or microscopic living things that drift along near the surface of the sea, and in freshwater.

Predator
An animal or microbe that hunts other creatures for food.

Prey
Anything caught by a predator.

Protist
All kinds of single-celled life, apart from bacteria. Protists include some species that behave like animals, some that live like plants, and some that are like both.

Root nodule
A growth on plant's root in which bacteria live. The bacteria change nitrogen from air in the soil into a form that the plant can use.

Sap
A liquid that carries nutrients in plants.

Species
A group of living things that look very similar, and can breed with each other but not with anything else.

Spores
Tiny packages of cells that are used in reproduction. Spores are like seeds, but they are smaller and simpler.

Symbiosis
A partnership between two living things from different species.

Thermophiles
Microbes that are specially adapted for survival at high temperatures.

Toxin
A substance made by one species that can poison another. Disease-causing bacteria often cause harm by releasing toxins in the body.

Virus
A package of chemicals that can copy itself by invading living cells.

Vitamin
A naturally occurring chemical that living things need to stay healthy.

Zooplankton
Small animals and animal-like organisms in plankton that live by eating food.

INDEX

CREDITS

Dorling Kindersley would like to thank:
Dean Price for jacket design and Chris Bernstein for the index.

Additional photography by:
Geoff Brightling, Andy Crawford, Neil Fletcher, Peter Gardner, Ian O'Leary, Dave King, Matthew Ward.

Models made by:
Chris Reynolds (BBC), Peter Minister, Dave Morgan, Gary Staab, Peter Griffiths.